STRAIGHT TALK ABOUT DRUGS

Drugs and
Medicines DM 68
LIFECRAFT

CompCare Publishers

2415 Annapolis Lane
Minneapolis, Minnesota 55441

Library of Congress Cataloging-in-Publication Data

Hewett, Paul.
    Straight talk about drugs / Paul Hewett.
      p. 48 cm.
    ISBN 0-89638-208-7
    1. Drug abuse—Popular works. 2. Psychotropic drugs—Popular
works. I. Title.
    RC564.29.H49 1990   89-20969
    362.29—dc20   CIP

Cover design by Jeremy Gale

Inquiries, orders, and catalog requests should be addressed to
CompCare Publishers
2415 Annapolis Lane
Minneapolis, MN 55441
Call toll free 800/328-3330
Minnesota residents 612/559-4800

  5   4   3   2   1
94   93   92   91   90

About the Author

Paul C. Hewett, Wilmette, Illinois, is a substance abuse counselor and national certified employee assistance professional, who is also trained in clinical pastoral education. He is associate director of ARCHEUS, an organization that provides employee assistance programs for several national companies, as well as firms in Illinois and New York.

Following his 1948 graduation from Georgetown University, he remained in Washington, D.C., for fifteen years, working with the National Security Agency and Technical Operations, Inc., before moving to Illinois to join the Caywood-Schiller Division of A.T. Kearney, Inc., Chicago.

He has been in the field of alcoholism and other drug abuse since 1972. He was industrial coordinator at the treatment center at Northwestern Memorial Hospital's Institute of Psychiatry for six years, then deputy director at the Martha Washington Hospital treatment center for four years.

He has served as president of the Illinois Chapter of Association of Labor-Management Administrators and Consultants on Alcoholism (ALMACA); as vice chair of the Bishop's Advisory Commission on Alcohol and Drugs for the Diocese of Chicago; as president of the Illinois Certification Board for Alcoholism Counselors (in 1987-88); and as board president, since 1986, of Cathedral Shelter of Chicago, a halfway house for alcoholics.

In 1980 he earned his M.Div. from Seabury-Western Theological Seminary in Evanston, Illinois, and has been associated with four Chicago area churches: Church of the Holy Spirit, Lake Forest, and St. Augustine's Church in Wilmette, as priest associate; St. Andrew's Church in Evanston and St. Alban's Church in Chicago, as priest-in-charge.

He has taught at National College of Education, Chicago, Evanston, and Lombard; at Seabury-Western Seminary, and at Central YMCA Community College in Chicago.

His professional memberships include ALMACA, Illinois Addictions Counselor Certification Board, Illinois Substance Abuse Counselor Certification Board, Illinois Certification Board for Alcoholism Counselors, Illinois Addiction Counselors Association, and Recovered Alcoholic Clergy Association.

Paul and his wife, Marion, married in 1948 and have seven grown children.

Introduction

Aspirin is a drug. So are acetaminophen and ibuprofen. But no doubt you know that already. The point is that the vast majority of the population *doesn't* know that. "Drug" to most people means "illegal drug"—heroin, crack, marijuana, and the like. The notion that prescription pharmaceuticals, over-the-counter preparations, nicotine, caffeine, and alcohol are *all* drugs is percolating into the national consciousness, but almighty slowly.

My goal in these brief definitions is not to tell you what you already know, but to fill you in on what the drug terms you hear really mean—as well as on what *some* people think they mean. It is also to sensitize you to count in nicotine and caffeine, alcohol, and over-the-counter and prescription medications when you think about (or total up) your own drug use or somebody else's.

While we're talking about drugs, just what is drug abuse? Is it abuse when *you* do it, but not when *I* do it? Drug abuse is a fuzzy term; it seems to mean whatever the one who says it wants it to mean.

Let's try this definition on for size: *drug abuse is the use of a mind-altering chemical in such a way as to present a risk of danger to the user or to someone else.*

That broad definition seems to cover drugged or drunk driving and drug overdoses. "Danger to the user" even covers what can happen when you get drunk or "high" in the privacy of your home. To get plastered or

1

wasted or stoned or high, to go to a kegger and overdo it, *is* to overdose on a drug. And overdoses certainly are instances of drug abuse.

Drug abuse can mean drug overuse or it can mean drug use, depending on the drug and the situation. The Addiction Research Foundation says that seven cups or less of coffee per day is okay. On the other hand, the U.S. Surgeon General says that *any* drinking of alcohol during pregnancy can harm the fetus. The line between drug use and abuse varies from drug to drug. But make absolutely no mistake: if a drug can affect your mind or damage you physically, ANY USE CAN BE ABUSE. *All* drugs can become drugs of abuse!

"Ignorance is no excuse," you hear. And ignorance about whether or not a substance is a drug—as well as whether it is illegal or not and what it can or might do to you—doesn't let you off the hook when it comes to the consequences of using it.

The following brief explanations may clarify some of the blurred information we often get about drugs, as well as some of the misconceptions we may have developed on our own.

Addicting Drug

Technically, addiction refers to a condition that is apparent when one stops doing "it" or taking "it," whatever "it" is. That is, addiction is synonymous with *physical* dependence, resulting in adverse physical withdrawal symptoms when the drug is taken away.

However, in ordinary conversation—and in some legislative bodies—the words "addiction," "dependence," and occasionally "use" (as in heroin use) often are casually interchanged.

For most practical purposes, continued use of a drug in the face of serious persistent problems associated with its use indicates addiction, or, if you prefer, dependence.

Under this definition, *all* drugs are addicting. You can become addicted to nasal inhalants, for example, destroying mucous tissue in the process.

The *physical* addiction to a drug like heroin or alcohol usually can be broken fairly quickly—in a matter of weeks. But overcoming *psychological* addiction or dependence is a lot tougher. Whether the addiction is physical or psychological or both, addiction is addiction.

Go ahead and ask a recovering alcoholic about "just one drink," or a former cocaine user about "just one more line"—ever! Ask a former smoker if it's possible to go back to "one and only one" cigarette after dinner. The Surgeon General proclaimed recently that nicotine is one of the most powerfully addicting drugs we know.

But *all* mind-altering drugs have the potential to be addicting. If it can affect my mind, there's a chance I'll become dependent on the sensations the drug produces, which is another way of saying "addicted." Before you fool with a drug, ask yourself, "Can I afford to gamble on the chance that I won't become addicted to this one—AND THEN FIND OUT I'M WRONG?" Mind-altering or intoxicating, mood-altering or psycho-tropic—it's all the same!

Believe me, recovery from drug (including alcohol) addiction is not easy. It is a lifelong process. And it's one that many fail.

Dangerous Drug

All mind-altering drugs are dangerous. A dose of pure snow or horse (heroin) can shock your heart into stopping. Angel dust or glue-sniffing can cause permanent brain damage. The questionable content of the so-called "designer drugs" can bring on neurological symptoms of Parkinson's disease. LSD can cause birth defects or sterility, they say. Sniffing cocaine can eat away the inside of your nose. Even alcohol can cause birth defects (Fetal Alcohol Effects or the full-blown Fetal Alcohol Syndrome). Too much aspirin will kill you, and so will too much of many other substances we think of as harmless. But you probably know all that—if you've been awake at all during the past ten years or so.

I believe there's a real danger in the term "dangerous drug," not because the drugs called dangerous aren't (THEY ARE!), but because the drugs *not* termed dangerous are considered harmless (AND THEY AREN'T!).

Some of us know, because we've had to deal with the casualties, that the drugs sometimes thought of as "harmless" (or, at least, less harmful than others)—like marijuana, tobacco, and alcohol—kill more people each year than all of the dangerous drugs you can come up with. Make no mistake, if a drug can affect your mind, it *is* dangerous, no matter what some folks say. And if it doesn't affect your mind, it has little appeal; you can't get high or mellow or hallucinate on it.

5

Depressant Drug

Depressant drugs, or "downers," operate on the central nervous system by depressing it, anesthetizing it, putting it to sleep. Although the term "high" means different things to different people, actually no one in history ever got high—that is, stimulated—from a depressant. You get quieted down, that's what you get! And if you take too many, or if you mix your downers, you'll get so quiet it'll take Gabriel himself to wake you!

The depressant family is very large. It includes various forms of barbiturates and other sedatives, minor tranquilizers such as Valium or Librium, and ethyl alcohol or ethanol (good old John Barleycorn himself!).

Some people take a depressant to feel better when they are blue. In fact, some clinically depressed people self-medicate with depressants. They couldn't be more wrong since, when the drug wears off, they become bluer—more "down"—than ever. For every three suicides in this country, one is found to be under the influence of alcohol, and another has taken some other kind of depressant. In other words, two out of three suicides are carried out under the influence of depressants!

Depressants also interact with one another, in a process termed *synergy*, or *potentiation*. This means that the effects of combining alcohol and, say, Valium are greater than the sum of the effects of both drugs taken separately—sort of a 2 + 2 = 6 phenomenon. This is how, as I understand it, Elvis Presley and

Marilyn Monroe and a host of others have died. *Very* dangerous stuff to mess with, these depressants!

Designer Drug

Some of the cleverest (and most conscienceless) chemists in the world "work the streets" to create drugs for an ever-increasing market. Our rich uncle, the one with the beard and the striped pants, passed laws controlling certain drugs by restricting access to them or, in some cases, prohibiting them altogether. So these enterprising chemists constructed new chemical compounds which are similar to, but slightly different from these controlled substances, and therefore not illegal. Since "designer jeans" were all the rage at the time, these deadly new drugs became glamorized, unfortunately, by the term "designer drugs."

The government, I am informed, has now closed that particular loophole, but there are many of these designer drugs around. These drugs have not been through the exhaustive process the Feds require of new medications, and their side effects are not completely known. One designer drug, for instance, induces Parkinsonism in those who take it even for a short period of time; and Parkinsonism is not reversible.

One designer drug, "crystal meth," has appeared in smokeable form, and is called "crank" on the street. This drug is even more dangerous than crack.

Anyone who will buy and take a drug whose effects are not known makes a powerful, negative statement about life, living, and self-esteem!

Gateway Drug

A gateway drug is a drug that is alleged to open the door to drug abuse, an introduction to the desperate world of the junkie. At various times and in various places, marijuana and alcohol have come under attack as gateway drugs. BALONEY! At this time, almost without a quibble within the chemical dependency field, the gateway drug is thought to be nicotine!

When a high school senior smokes cigarettes, the probability of his or her using another drug (not counting caffeine) is three times higher than if the senior doesn't smoke. That convinces me! How about you?

Hallucinogenic Drug
(Psychedelic Drug)

The name tells you all you need to know about this family of drugs. They cause hallucinations. Sometimes these psychedelics, as they are also called, appear to scramble your sensory circuits, so that users report "seeing" sounds or "hearing" colors. They send you on a hallucinatory "trip." If you are looking forward without fear to the experience, you may have a "good trip." If you are afraid or reluctant, you may have a "bad trip." Sometimes you have a bad trip *anyway*, no matter what your attitude is.

There are two very important and serious side effects of hallucinogenic drugs. First, they are lipid-soluble, which means that they dissolve and are stored in fatty tissue. Thus it is possible to have a "flashback" long after you believe the effects of the drug have worn off. This could be anything from embarrassing to highly dangerous, depending on what you're doing at the time of the flashback. Some authorities claim that flashbacks are psychological and can take place even when there's none of the drug left in you, which is even *more* scary.

Second, regular use of one of these drugs, angel dust (PCP, or phencyclidine), can cause permanent brain damage. Now, dust can be fixed up to mimic many other drugs, including the rest of the psychedelics. But dust is a whole lot easier and cheaper to prepare than, say, acid (LSD or lysergic acid diethylamide). And the user can't tell the difference. So, much of the drug sold as LSD on the street isn't; it's dust.

All this PLUS the fact that, while under the influence of these drugs, one may believe that one can fly, and step off a roof—or that one is faster than a speeding bullet, and jaywalk in freeway traffic.

These hallucinogens or psychedelics scare the bejabbers out of me! A Supreme Court decision on obscenity used the defining phrase "having no redeeming social value." On that basis, these drugs are obscene!

Hard Drug

I suppose that the term "hard drug" was coined by someone to justify using another drug which, of course, was not "hard." It usually applies to drugs like heroin, cocaine, and amphetamines.

I use the term in a different way, partly because I don't want to suggest that the use of any drug, "hard" or "soft," is harmless, and partly because I want to call a spade a bloody shovel! As I—and many others—use it, the term hard drug means one that CAN CAUSE DEATH FROM A SINGLE INCIDENCE OF USE. "Wow! You mean just once and it's all over?" No, what I mean is both better and worse. Better, because most people most of the time don't die when they use a hard drug. Worse, because some of them do, and you never know when one of these drugs can cause you to die.

What I mean by a hard drug is that use of it is a form of Russian roulette. When you use a powerful drug, it can be a heck of a jolt to the body. Your heart may quit. You may forget to breathe. You may smother. You may strangle in your own vomit or on your own tongue. You may bleed to death because you feel no pain. You may drive your car up a tree or attempt to clean out the clientele in a bar single-handed. There are many ways to "wake up dead."

By the way, when I say powerful, I really mean it. An effective dose of LSD is roughly one ten-billionth your body weight. How little is a ten-billionth? Look at it this way: a dose of LSD equivalent to the amount of aspirin in two tablets (650 mg) is enough to get well over a million people stoned! That's powerful!

Illegal Drug

One wonders whether to be amused or enraged by high-sounding concerns, voiced at all levels, about "illegal drugs." Amused first, perhaps, because the term illegal drug is so vague, it's meaningless. Consider these facts:

- Valium is an *illegal drug* for you if it was not prescribed for you, but perfectly legal for me if it was prescribed for me.

- Alcohol is an *illegal drug:*

    in certain parts of this country, such as "dry" counties;

    while performing certain acts, such as driving a car or working at certain jobs;

    to purchase at certain times of the day, such as 6 A.M. in Chicago;

    for anyone under twenty-one years of age.

- Tobacco is an illegal drug:

    in certain forms, as in pipes and cigars on airplanes;

    in certain places, as in most movie theaters and on short plane flights;

    for all people under a certain age (this varies from place to place).

Yet tobacco is also legal at almost all times and ages in the form of "smokeless tobacco."

Although I'm amused by these ridiculous inconsistencies, I am, at the same time, enraged because I believe we are losing the "war on drugs." This is happening as much through bureaucratic maneuvering as through public apathy. I am also enraged because our self-righteous concerns about drugs are so often expressed hypocritically, with cocktail glass and cigarette in hand. Or by a celebrity who's busted on drug charges a few days or weeks later—or who's advertising some form of booze on the same TV channel! I am enraged because the concern seems to be the "illegal" aspects and not the "drug" itself that are in public focus. The person who's into crack or angel dust or crystal meth is much more a mortality statistic waiting to happen than a criminal! I cannot help but feel that if we could only take away the drug, the illegal part would take care of itself—and fade away.

Finally, I am amused because who knows what substance will be illegal or legal fifty years from now. At one time or another, in one place or another, both chocolate and coffee were illegal drugs. And at one time in Russia, possession of tobacco could cost you your head!

Immoral Drug

The term "immoral drug" may not be heard often outside of some churches, but what the term indicates about our national attitudes ought to be examined. It is clear that inanimate objects such as drugs cannot have "morality" and therefore cannot be immoral. It is also clear that what one society sees as immoral may be seen as perfectly righteous in another society. For example, Tutankhamen, because his blood was thought to be divine and therefore not to be mixed with ordinary human blood, was *morally* obligated to marry his sister—something nearly every other society has labeled immoral.

We all know that, don't we? And yet there is a moral flavor to our attitude toward the drug user, the drug abuser, and, above all, the drug dealer. Sometimes we exhibit traces of a moralistic attitude toward alcohol and tobacco, both legal drugs. Think a minute . . . . What do we call alcohol and tobacco taxes? That's right—"sin taxes!"

This is not the forum to bring into debate questions of right and wrong about drug abuse; these are complex issues, and not getting any simpler. But please remember that drugs, of themselves, are not moral or immoral— even though the behavior they bring about in the user, the abuser, or the addict may very well be immoral.

Legal Drug

A legal drug, as its name implies, is one a person may take legally. By implication, there are ordinarily legal controls governing its use, except for recent loopholes, as in the case of designer drugs when they were first produced.

Valium, for example, is a legal drug only when prescribed by a physician. On the other hand, the controls on alcohol or tobacco use have more to do with accessibility of the drug—limiting its use through rationing, licensing, age restrictions, or taxation.

Here, in the last few years of the twentieth century, in these oh-so-enlightened United States and in spite of our much publicized war on drugs, we still consider "legal" the consumption of alcohol and nicotine, which *kill* something on the order of 600,000 of us each year!

Tobacco use is blamed for more than a third of a million deaths per year, from cancer, emphysema, and other illnesses related to smoking. Alcohol-related motor vehicle accidents kill more of our most valuable resource—our young people—each year than any other kind of accident or illness. Alcohol and nicotine are *drugs*, highly addicting drugs, dangerous drugs, deadly drugs—and yet legal drugs. In the case of these two drugs, maybe we should spell legal *l-e-t-h-a-l*!

Narcotic Drug

The federal government and several state legislatures, in their collective wisdom, have named all sorts of substances "narcotics," including marijuana, cocaine, and others. If it weren't indicative of a pervasive and frightening lack of knowledge on a serious subject, these misnomers might even be funny.

Narcotic means "sleep maker," and that's precisely what real narcotics do; they put you to sleep. Morphine—named for Morpheus, the Greek God of sleep—is a surgical anesthetic.

Look at the street terms for the effects of narcotics use—"nodding," "mellow," "the big sleep"—and you see that sleep is the key result of their use.

Statutes aside, narcotics come in just two kinds. Opiates, like heroin and codeine, are derivatives of the opium poppy. (Now you see why Dorothy, Toto, and the rest fell asleep in the poppy field outside the Emerald City of Oz!) Opioids, which include such substances as Dilaudid and Methadone, are chemicals that are not derived from opium but act as if they were.

There is a lesson in the name "heroin." The Bayer pharmaceutical company developed a "miracle drug" intended to cure the serious morphine addiction problem in the United States and Europe, especially among amputees who had fought in the Crimean and Civil wars. They came up with a "heroic" substance as a "cure" for our addicted war heroes. You guessed it—it was heroin! And the junkies simply exchanged masters, from morphine to heroin. The moral of the story is that the illness of drug addiction is not treated well or for long by the administration of other drugs.

We didn't learn much from this experience, but repeated it in more recent years by using Methadone— an opioid—to treat heroin addiction. And the junkies switched masters again!

These narcotic drugs, all of them, opioids and opiates alike, are highly addicting and very dangerous— definitely not to be taken lightly. Among the dangers of narcotic addiction are inadvertent overdose (which can be fatal), increased risk of exposure to hepatitis (the "iron mosquito"), AIDS, and generally heightened vulnerability to illness.

Over-the-Counter Drugs

Over-the-counter drugs, as long as you have the money to pay for them, are not restricted as to use. That is, one may purchase them over the counter at a drug store. Now, many of us seem to believe that anything we can buy as easily as a chocolate bar is no more a threat to our health and safety than a chocolate bar. And that is just plain WRONG!

There are, for example, several cold remedies available over the counter that have more alcohol content than any wine sold in this country, as well as versions of these medications for "daytime" use which are stronger than most beers! These preparations may also contain other medicines, such as acetaminophen.

Most diet preparations, even those that are marked "no caffeine," contain PPA or phenylpropanolamine. PPA has pretty much the same effect on the body as drugs in the stimulant family (amphetamines and cocaine are stimulants). Some people are abusing PPA, or have become dependent upon it.

For the careful consumer, there are two rules about over-the-counter drugs:

1. READ THE LABEL. Know what you're taking and what it does to your body. (After all, it's the only one you'll ever have!)

2. FOLLOW THE INSTRUCTIONS. That's why they're provided. And note that most of these preparations have provisions for handling abuse

and overdose situations; they're included here for plenty of good reasons!

Prescription Drug

Prescription drugs are controlled substances, in that there are statutory restrictions on who may order their use, how they may be provided, and to whom, and so on. Usually this means that a physician writes a prescription that So-and-So may have so many tablets of Brand X in such-and-such strength, to be taken so many times per day. Some medicines also have a restriction on the number of times a prescription may be filled.

It should be obvious that, if these drugs are so potentially dangerous that their use is controlled by the authorities, there is grave risk of abuse. And such is the case. For example, amphetamines, morphine, codeine, and all benzodiazapines (including Valium and Librium) are prescription drugs. All are described in other parts of this pamphlet as dangerous drugs, and even in some circumstances as illegal drugs.

There are two cautions about prescription drugs:

1. READ THE LABEL ON THE PRESCRIP-TION. It will tell you when and how to take it. Follow these instructions; again, there are good reasons why they are there. The label also may warn you not to drive or drink alcohol while taking the medication. Follow these instructions. If you don't, the best that can be said is that you are *abusing* these drugs.

2. IF YOU ARE TAKING A PRESCRIPTION

OF SOME SORT, AND YOU WONDER IF IT'S SAFE TO DRINK ALCOHOL WHILE TAKING IT, ASK YOUR PHARMACIST, not your doctor—unless you have a very enlightened physician. Your druggist has had four years of pharmacology. Your medic may have had no more than two semesters!

Psychedelic Drug

Good-sounding names seem to take the sting out of unpleasantness and negativity. A military retreat becomes a "retrograde movement." An economic depression becomes a "recession." And a garbage collector becomes a "sanitary engineer."

So it is, I believe, that hallucinogenic drugs came to be called "psychedelic drugs." Since these drugs cause the user to have hallucinations, and hallucinations may be unpleasant things to have—scary and abnormal and unpredictable—the term "psychedelic" seems to gloss over the negatives and glamorize them. Psychedelic was also associated with the sensational colors, the strobes, the hip clothes, and the wild posters that were part of the sixties' youth mystique. This hip, modern, young aura rubbed off on this family of drugs. Although the colors and sounds of the sixties are long gone, the psychedelic—or hallucinogenic—drugs are still around making trouble.

The truth is that these drugs—LSD and angel dust and mushroom (psilocybin) and peyote—are not glamorous. They are dangerous drugs, hard drugs, hallucinogenic drugs, and, as I said before, obscene drugs! (See "Hallucinogenic Drugs").

Recreational Drug

Another way to minimize drug use is by giving it a "nice" name. Recreation is essential. It is healthy. It is good for you. So, by implication, recreational drug use is "okay" use.

Well, if there is drug use that is thought to be okay, then there must be drugs that are also thought to be okay because they are used for recreation. WRONG—THIS DOESN'T FOLLOW!

How about your morning coffee? Recreational use of caffeine? And what about the way most people use alcohol? Recreational? But because some people use caffeine or nicotine "recreationally," it doesn't mean that all use of these drugs is for recreation.

Alcohol, as you hardly need to be reminded, is a dangerous drug, a hard drug. To the alcoholic and the alcohol abuser, it is a life-threatening drug.

Moreover, the mere fact that I'm fooling around with a drug, using it for "play," doesn't rationalize or legitimize its use. A toot of cocaine is not recreational, but a grim game of chance. You may believe you're "playing" with a drug, but you can be sure that the drug dealer you get it from, legally or otherwise, is not in business for his recreation or his health—or yours either.

Soft Drug

The "soft drugs"—unlike the hard ones like cocaine, heroin, and alcohol—usually don't pose a risk of death upon a single incidence of use. There *is* a risk of death following a single incidence of use, but it is far more likely to occur from cumulative effects of long-term use.

Drugs in this category are tobacco, caffeine, and marijuana. Heavy and/or protracted use of any of the three is very dangerous. Tobacco is not only one of the most addictive substances known, but the diseases related to its use make it the leading cause of death in the United States. Marijuana smoke is twenty times the cancer hazard of tobacco smoke!

Marijuana also is known to cause liver damage, reduced sperm count, diminished mental capacity, memory lapse, and a host of other disorders.

Long-time caffeine use (over seven cups per day) increases the risk of stomach, kidney, and bladder cancer, as well as a variety of gastrointestinal disorders.

Make no mistake, just because a drug is labeled soft doesn't mean it can't be deadly!

Stimulant Drug

Stimulants are drugs that pep up the central nervous system. These are the drugs that get you high. That is, your blood pressure, pulse, body temperature, and respiration all go up.

This is exactly what happens when you stumble into the kitchen in the morning and have the first pop of the day, be it coffee or tea. Stimulant drugs include caffeine, which is the active ingredient in coffee, tea, and chocolate, as well as some colas. Does this mean that "high breakfast" (as opposed to "high tea") is made up of cola and a chocolate bar? Ugh!

Amphetamines (speed) and cocaine are also stimulants, or uppers. Phenylpropanolamine (PPA), available in diet medications, behaves much like other stimulants and like them can produce abuse and dependence.

Now all drugs have possible side effects, and stimulants are no exception. Chief among these side effects are loss of appetite (there is often a relationship between use of stimulants and anorexia) and loss of sleep (insomnia or inability to sleep).

Sleeping and eating involve fundamental body rhythms, and protracted interference with these cycles can cause psychotic-like reactions. In a phrase, doing uppers for too long can make you act crazy. Overdoing uppers also may *kill* you! Specific mechanisms include cardiac arrest, tachycardia, rapid heartbeat, and other heart anomalies, as well as stroke and respiratory arrest.

Any preparation to "help you stay awake,"

whether an over-the-counter or prescription drug, is helping your body overcome, or at least put off, its natural desire to sleep. This is stimulation by another name, and abuse of these preparations has the same effect as abuse of cocaine or speed. Believe it!

Nicotine kills directly; I am told that a drop of pure nicotine on the skin will kill a rabbit in ten seconds. But humans die more from the effects of the several hundred-odd other things in tobacco smoke than from the drug nicotine, to which they are addicted.

Street Drug

The term "street drug" is used to refer to drugs bought on the street, that is, illegally. There are three sorts of street drugs.

First is the prohibited drug—the drug no one (except a few researchers) may possess legally. This includes heroin, cocaine and crack, marijuana, LSD, angel dust, and others.

The next group is made up of legal drugs illegally purchased, including codeine, morphine, Valium, and other prescription drugs. A side note: a 10 mg Valium tablet, which is blue, is called a "blue martini" on the street because it will hit you just about as hard as a conventional drink of the same name.

Third are the cooked-up concoctions, the "welfare drugs," such as Talwin and Pyribenzamine, otherwise known as "T's and blues," or Doriden and quarter-grain codeine cough syrup ("Dors and fours"), which imitate heroin and other opiates.

In general, the tone of the term street drug is one of DANGER. Newspapers and television news programs are full of stories about drug-related crime, much of it linked with "crack" or "rock," a ready-mixed freebased cocaine. The person hooked on a street drug is also susceptible to death in quicker forms than from the drug alone.

Before buying a drug on the street, consider the following:

1. You don't know what you're buying, because the seller doesn't know what he or she is selling. I don't care if your connection is your mother (and I have had clients whose connections *were* their mothers!), you don't know what you bought. You may *think* you know, and you may be right, but you don't know for sure.

2. You don't know how strong it is. The more desirable and/or expensive the drug is originally, the more you can be certain that it has been cut, or "stepped on" in order to maximize profits. What you don't know is how often and how hard it's been stepped on.

Here, stop and think a minute. If you don't know what you bought or how strong it is, *there is no way in Hades to figure out in advance what the dose is going to do to you!* And that's not the worst of it! Read on to Number 3.

3. The worst news is that you don't know what it's been cut with. If your heroin is 3 percent pure, it's 97 percent something else. Some samples of drugs have been cut with innocuous substances, such as milk sugar. Others have been cut with talcum powder, which is a long way from innocuous when introduced into the blood stream. Marijuana samples have been found to be contaminated with paraquat, which causes cancer in humans, as well as fungus and mold spores. And so on.

4. The bad news goes on. There are crazies out there who believe that people who use drugs should

die, and decide to help them do just that. In a recent year in Chicago, we found human feces, ground glass, arsenic, and rat poison in drug samples submitted for analysis.

In summary, one way or another, you are taking your life in your hands when you buy a drug on the street!

Useless (Useful) Drug

Often, drugs are described in terms of their "usefulness" or "uselessness" to society. The truth is that there are legitimate medical uses for many of the drugs popularly damned in the media. Heroin penetrates the "blood-brain barrier" more readily than morphine and, therefore, is a more effective and humane pain killer for terminally ill cancer patients. Marijuana is effective in treating glaucoma and in countering the nausea often associated with chemotherapy. Cocaine is an excellent surface anesthetic, and is quite useful in eye surgery.

The fact that a drug is "useful" in some way does not mean it is not also a possible drug of abuse.

There may even be a legitimate use for nicotine, although I admit I can't think of it right now!

To Summarize . . .

Here are some thoughts to leave with you:

1. IF IT CAN AFFECT YOUR MIND, IT IS DANGEROUS!

2. IF YOU "NEED" A DRUG, YOU'RE A DRUG-ABUSER.

3. DRUG ABUSE IS NOT GLAMOROUS OR COOL. IT'S LETHAL.

And, above all:

4. IGNORANCE ABOUT DRUGS CAN KILL YOU.